CONTENTS

SPORTS

ARCHERY7
BASEBALL I8
BASEBALL II9
BASEBALL III10
BASEBALL IV11
BODYBUILDING I12
BODYBUILDING II13
BOXING14
FISHING I15
FISHING II16
FISHING III17
FOOTBALL I18
FOOTBALL II19
FOOTBALL III20
HOCKEY21
HUNTING I22
HUNTING II23
RAQUETBALL24
SAILING25
SKIING I26
SKIING II27
SKI BUNNY28
SOCCER I29
SOCCER II30
SURFING I31
SURFING II32
SWIMMING33
SWIMMING/MERMAID34
TENNIS I35
TENNIS II36
TENNIS III37
VOLLEYBALL38
WATERSKIING I39
WATERSKIING II40
WATERSKIING III41
WATERSKIING IV42
WRESTLING43

HOBBIES

ARTIST47
AEROBICS48
BEACH/SUNTANNING49
BOATS50
DANCING/PARTYING51
DANCING52
DRINKING I53
DRINKING II54
DRIVING I55
DRIVING II56
DRIVING III57
GAMBLING I58
GAMBLING II59
HORSEBACK RIDING I60
HORSEBACK RIDING II61
KNITTING62
PETS/WALKING DOG I63
PETS/WALKING DOG II64
PIANO65
READING66
SAILING67
SINGING68
TRUMPET69
SHOPPING I70
SHOPPING II71
SEWING72

CONTENTS

PROFESSIONS

BOSS 75
BUSINESSMAN/SALES 76
CARPENTER 77
COMPUTER 78
DENTAL HYGIENE 79
DOCTOR 80
GUITAR 81
HAIRDRESSER 82
LAWYER 83
MAKING MONEY 84
MILITARY/HELICOPTER 85

MILITARY/NAVY 86
MILITARY/PARACHUTE 87
MILITARY/TANK 88
MILITARY/RAMBO 89
NURSE 90
REAL ESTATE 91
SALESMAN 92
SECRETARY 93
SINGING 94
SURGEON 95

KIDS ONLY

BABIES/BOTTLE 99
BABIES/CRAWLING 100
BABIES/SWIMMING 101
BALLET 102
BICYCLE 103
CHASING BOYS 104
DEVIL 105
GYMNASTICS 106
NINTENDO 107

PETS I 108
PETS II 109
ROLLERSKATING 110
SKATEBOARDING I 111
SKATEBOARDING II 112
TRICYCLE 113
TROUBLE 114
VIDEO ARCADE 115

INTRODUCTION

Coming up with gag ideas on the spot can be a nerve-wracking experience. That is why this book was created ~ to aid you with ideas so that you do not have to go through that kind of ordeal.

There is, literally, an infinite amount of gag jokes you can use. What I have compiled here are 100 or so drawing that you, the caricaturist, can refer to and use as a beginning arsenal. Mix and match bodies, signs, thought bubbles to your own liking. Use this book as a springboard for your own ideas. Copy the drawings and memorize them. Pretty soon you will get the idea on how to put any gag together, even the most obscure profession. Remember, practicing over and over makes the process go faster and easier. Draw as many objects you can from memory and life. Keep a file of cartoons that seem to solve drawing problems of difficult objects. It's also a good idea to maintain a file of photographs of various objects for referral.

I wish you much luck and fortune in your caricaturing endeavors.
Happy drawing!

Sincerely,

Jim van der Keyl

SPORTS

ARCHERY

SPORTS

BASEBALL 1

SPORTS

BASEBALL II

SPORTS

BASEBALL III

SPORTS

BASEBALL IV

SPORTS

BODYBUILDING I

SPORTS

BODYBUILDING II

SPORTS

BOXING

SPORTS

FISHING I

SPORTS

FISHING II

SPORTS

FISHING III

SPORTS

FOOTBALL 1

SPORTS

FOOTBALL II

SPORTS

FOOTBALL III

SPORTS

HOCKEY

SPORTS

HUNTING 1

SPORTS

HUNTING II

SPORTS

RAQUETBALL

SPORTS

SAILING

SPORTS

SKIING I

SPORTS

SKIING II

SPORTS

SKI BUNNY

SPORTS

SOCCER 1

SPORTS

Soccer II

SPORTS

SURFING 1

SPORTS

SURFING II

SPORTS

SWIMMING

SPORTS

SWIMMING/MERMAID

SPORTS

TENNIS 1

35

SPORTS

TENNIS II

SPORTS

TENNIS III

SPORTS

VOLLEYBALL

SPORTS

WATERSKIING 1

SPORTS

WATERSKIING II

SPORTS

WATERSKIING III

SPORTS

WATERSKIING IV

SPORTS

WRESTLING

HOBBIES

HOBBIES

ARTIST

HOBBIES

AEROBICS

HOBBIES

BEACH/SUNTANNING

HOBBIES

BOATS

HOBBIES

DANCING/PARTYING

HOBBIES

DANCING

HOBBIES

DRINKING 1

HOBBIES

DRINKING II

HOBBIES

DRIVING I

HOBBIES

DRIVING II

HOBBIES

DRIVING III

HOBBIES

GAMBLING I

HOBBIES

GAMBLING II

HOBBIES

HORSEBACK RIDING 1

HOBBIES

HORSEBACK RIDING II

HOBBIES

KNITTING

HOBBIES

PETS/WALKING THE DOG 1

HOBBIES

PETS/WALKING THE DOG II

HOBBIES

PIANO

HOBBIES

READING

HOBBIES

SAILING

HOBBIES

SINGING

HOBBIES

TRUMPET

HOBBIES

SHOPPING I

HOBBIES

SHOPPING II

HOBBIES

SEWING

PROFESSIONS

BOSS

PROFESSIONS

BUSINESSMAN/SALES

PROFESSIONS

CARPENTER

PROFESSIONS

COMPUTER

PROFESSIONS

DENTAL HYGIENE

PROFESSIONS

DOCTOR

PROFESSIONS

GUITAR

PROFESSIONS

HAIRDRESSER

PROFESSIONS

LAWYER

PROFESSIONS

MAKING MONEY

PROFESSIONS

MILITARY/HELICOPTER

PROFESSIONS

MILITARY/NAVY

PROFESSIONS

MILITARY/PARACHUTE

PROFESSIONS

MILITARY/TANK

PROFESSIONS

MILITARY/RAMBO

PROFESSIONS

NURSE

PROFESSIONS

REAL ESTATE

PROFESSIONS

SALESMAN

PROFESSIONS

SECRETARY

PROFESSIONS

SINGING

PROFESSIONS

SURGEON

KID'S ONLY

KID'S ONLY

BABIES/BOTTLE

KID'S ONLY

BABIES/CRAWLING

KiD'S ONLY

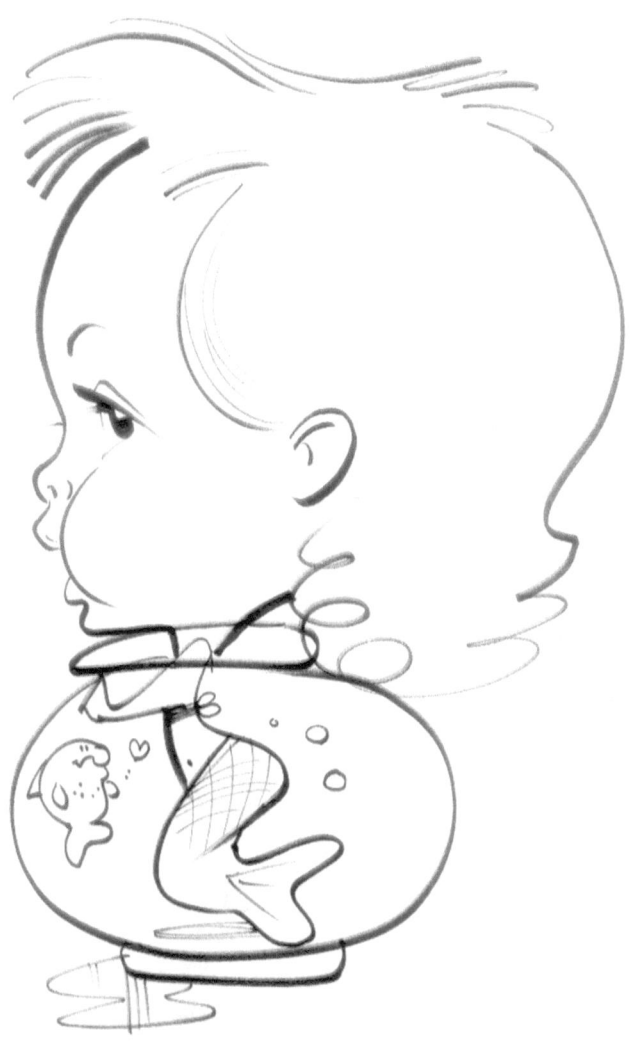

BABIES/SWIMMING/WATER

KID'S ONLY

BALLET

KID'S ONLY

BICYCLE

KID'S ONLY

CHASING BOYS

KID'S ONLY

DEVIL

KID'S ONLY

GYMNASTICS

KID'S ONLY

NINTENDO

KID'S ONLY

PETS

KID'S ONLY

PETS II

KID'S ONLY

ROLLERSKATING

KID'S ONLY

SKATEBOARDING 1

KID'S ONLY

SKATEBOARDING II

KID'S ONLY

TRICYCLE

KID'S ONLY

TROUBLE

KID'S ONLY

VIDEO ARCADE

www.ingramcontent.com/pod-product-compliance
Lightning Source LLC
Chambersburg PA
CBHW022022170526
45157CB00003B/1322